Simple Poems, Simple Truths of a Simple Life

SIMPLY Free

MICHAEL G. HOGAN

abbott press

This book is a work of non-fiction. Unless otherwise noted, the author and the publisher make no explicit guarantees as to the accuracy of the information contained in this book and in some cases, names of people and places have been altered to protect their privacy.

Abbott Press books may be ordered through booksellers or by contacting:

Abbott Press
1663 Liberty Drive
Bloomington, IN 47403
www.abbottpress.com
Phone: 1 (866) 697-5310

Because of the dynamic nature of the Internet, any web addresses or links contained in this book may have changed since publication and may no longer be valid. The views expressed in this work are solely those of the author and do not necessarily reflect the views of the publisher, and the publisher hereby disclaims any responsibility for them.

Any people depicted in stock imagery provided by Thinkstock are models, and such images are being used for illustrative purposes only. Certain stock imagery © Thinkstock.

ISBN: 978-1-4582-2136-0 (sc)
ISBN: 978-1-4582-2223-7 (hc)
ISBN: 978-1-4582-2137-7 (e)

Library of Congress Control Number: 2017913935

Print information available on the last page.

Abbott Press rev. date: 01/23/2019

CONTENTS

DEDICATION

*This book is dedicated to my father. He suffered
from a terrible disease of alcoholism.
I can only think he is finally at peace after his passing
many years ago and setting his demons free.
No one realizes how very much I have missed
him, his teachings, his guidance, his humor.
To my mother whose steadfastness and raising 6 children
through living hard times is nothing short of a miracle.
She has been the one constant throughout my life.*

*To my wife Linda and my children Stacy,
Jennifer, and Scott, you are my life.
You are my reason for being. Thanks
so, so much!!! I love you all.*

*To our newest family arrival, Charlotte Quinn Hogan.
You have no idea how much you have
already touched our families.
You will be well guided and loved
more than you will know.
You have brought a new light into our hearts.
You are special, our Charlotte Quinn!*

PREFACE

Friends, let me start by thanking you for your interest in these simple words. I did not begin to write poems, I began to write things about my father. One poem led to two, then to three, and so on.

I really don't know how the words come to me, but the titles of each seem eerily easy and free flowing. These poems span a wide array of feelings, emotions, ideas, and whatever else came to mind at the time. I started in March of 2017 and by July had written all of these.

If you read them slowly, read them more than once, a story will appear for each, some for laughs, some to cry, and some for just why not. There are secrets here hidden in the words, truth's be told I guess. I'm not Whitman, or Emerson, or anyone else, just simply me.

These simple poems are from the heart, from the mind. I hope you enjoy them. There is more on the way.

Well who would have thought, more poems! Why? Just because I can. I love doing them, I love the hidden messages. Bucket list item? I don't know about that, it's just me. Once again more on the way.

A CHILD'S BURDEN

Why so loud when sleep time rolls
It's unstill in rooms they toll
There is talk, most unclear
No words, I'm scared and shed a tear

Morning fetch's calming air
Light brings happy thoughts to bare
No need to think about dark of night
It will come soon enough on twilight

Confusion is masked by play and fun
Night will bring some things undone
Mom is still, this night we'll tout
Dad is gone, he's out and about

When morning rolls we'll see the past
I only hope it won't last
I pray for something, confused I am
Why are nights just a sham?

Sleep again I'll try tonight
Please try less fright, with all my might
I rest on Mom each weary day
I just want to play and play

Oh Dad, oh Dad where are you now
I need to talk somewhere somehow
Oh Dad I miss you each day gone past
I just hope this does not last

THERE'S EVIL IN THE BOTTLE

Bottle to bottle, can to can
What evil lurks the dreadful plan
Drink my son, drink till you're numb
You must forget the day's humdrum

Evil comes inside the bottle
We all must test the tempted throttle
Fast we go through drink and time
More we take the more sublime

Oh evil now you grab me true
You guide through the times so blue
The mask you wear hides the truth
It all happened in my youth

The hunt began with friends and glee
Innocent and young were we
Shots rang out from which I thrilled
My friend has died, this one I killed

Bottle to Bottle, is my plan?
My solitude lives inside me man
I cannot bare the truth be told
An accident is how it sold

Each day I wish it could not be
My friend lies dead is all I see
My head throbs from guilt like hell
I pray this evil dies as well

No bottle, no can to lose myself in
Only a wish to stop my sin
And relish heaven and stars above
I pray so much for all I love

SOMETHINGS WRONG DAD

Like unsure steps in a mushy field
The feeling of doom won't soon yield
I pray these feelings will soon drown out
I press the nature of the doubt

Questions surround my spinning mind
This cannot be my dad, my own kind
What's happened to my idol true?
He was all knowing and now I am through

Dad oh Dad, how can it be
These changes to frequent for me to see
Come back, come back to what you were
Quiet my mind and slow the blur

It's hard for me the ebb and flows
One day is happy, then there's crows
Help me handle the ups and downs
I feel so confused like a swirly clown

Who are you dad you change too much
Like when you drink is that your crutch
What's in the bottle you crave so dearly?
It doesn't help me see you clearly

I pray, I pray for things to turn
Steady my mind from the churn
Only my Dad controls the change
Please Dad don't be so strange

TROUBLED MIND

My mind wanders like a leaf in the wind
Focus shifts from sin to sin
Steady my heart is only the path
Wind down my troubles sleep, sleep, sleep

Trouble, trouble, on my mind
All my soul to rest for time
Good deeds, good friends, is what I need
To quell the trouble my mind sees

Awaken now to new and crisp
Oh twist the sadness to paltry crumbs
Steady my heart on waters gone calm
Rest easy chum smooth rides ahead

Trouble, trouble, on my mind
All my soul to rest for a time
Good deeds, good friends, is what I need
To quell the trouble my mind sees

Trouble chases the porous mind
Take courage my friend from those before,
Those who traveled the treacherous road
Only to live on mountains top

Trouble, trouble, on my mind
All my soul to rest for a time
Good deeds, good friends, is what I need
To quell the trouble my mind sees

Troubled mind comes from within
The quakes of sin we'll crush again
My mind will settle and be set free
I only wait for it to be

Trouble, trouble, on my mind
All my soul to rest for a time
Good deeds, good friends, is what I need
To quell the trouble my mind sees

TIPPLERS ROAD

Winding down the tipplers road I toast the toad who's lost the load
Crossing down the steps of drink I only sail unto the brink
Oh save me now from the slew, I fear I'm falling nothing new

Swallow my troubles drink up, drink up,
Bury my troubles for none to see,
I've tried, I've tried to be set free only to travel this grisly sea
On Tipplers road I cannot see the troubles that are in front of me
Drink up, Drink up, I pray again, help me now, please help me again

Belly up to the bar, one more drink, that's all I will need before
the brink
Go dark my mind of blended things, confusion is what truly stings
One for the road is my cry, I'll have just one before I die

Swallow my troubles drink up, drink up,
Bury my troubles for none to see,
I've tried, I've tried to be set free only to travel this grisly sea
On Tipplers road I cannot see the troubles that are in front of me
Drink up, Drink up, I pray again, help me now, please help me again

There's hope ahead I truly think, it's just not in that one more drink
Settle me down, slow the bow, slow the turns, and ease my sins
Steady the road I travel too, guide me right, and guide me true

Swallow my troubles drink up, drink up,
Bury my troubles for none to see,
I've tried, I've tried to be set free only to travel this grisly sea
On Tipplers road I cannot see the troubles that are in front of me
Drink up, Drink up, I pray again, help me now, please help me again
For Tipplers road has got to be the place I really don't want to be

GOTTA GET IT NOW!!

—— ⚜ ——

I want it, I need it, can't you see, I gotta get it now
I crave to swallow one more dream, I have to forget what I've seen
Lose my soul, lose my heart, lost my mind in one small part

I gotta get it now, before I wake to see, the foul truth and all that be
Gotta get it now one more time before I fall into the crime
Gotta have it now, before my love can see that this is really, really me
Just help me get it now, help me stem the tide, slowly turn the ride
I gotta get it now, I gotta get it somehow

In the bottle is my home, peaceful dreams will stop my roam
One more flask of devils brew, it's gotta let my mind be true
Devil, devil, a drink with me, gives me comfort you will see

I gotta get it now, before I wake to see, the foul truth and all that be
Gotta get it now one more time before I fall into the crime
Gotta have it now, before my love can see that this is really, really me
Just help me get it now, help me stem the tide, slowly turn the ride
I gotta get it now, I gotta get it somehow

Burn, burn my souls on fire, yearning for that new desire
Help me turn my twisted disease, to the straight and narrow please
My quest is one of getting clean, quench my quivering soul to sheen

I gotta get it now, before I wake to see, the foul truth and all that be
Gotta get it now one more time before I fall into the crime
Gotta have it now, before my love can see that this is really, really me
Just help me get it now, help me stem the tide, slowly turn the ride
I gotta get it now, I gotta get it somehow

If I get it now will I be ready for the change, challenge my mind left strange
Steer me to the Promised Land, days of bliss and goodness at hand
Gotta get that happiness here and now, come hell or high water gotta get that vow?

I gotta get it now, before I wake to see, the foul truth and all that be
Gotta get it now one more time before I fall into the crime
Gotta have it now, before my love can see that this is really, really me
Just help me get it now, help me stem the tide, slowly turn the ride
I gotta get it now, I gotta get it somehow

LONELY IN A
CROWDED WORLD

Surrounded by clamor of the unwilling throng
I beckon for one to listen to my song
I can reach out and touch the splendid flock
But waver I do this all a crock

Loneliness grips my weary soul
It tears at my being, with this I roll
Hear my words on silent air
I beg for someone who may care

Standing as one in the midst of the crowd
Everything I ponder is just a shroud
Hear me, help me, I cry from within
But nothing responds to my chagrin

So die I might calls left unheeded
No one knew what I really needed
The wall from within is so mightily thick
Loneliness bests me none to the quick

Hear me, help me, silently I scream
On deaf ears my cries do gleam
For it is within the answer lies
I must reach out before it dies

LONELY SOUL

Gaze upon the stars so bright
Lonely I sit, my soul so tight
Dream I can, no substance in hand
Reach for comfort so far and bland

If only I could find the solace in thought
But these terrible things I have wrought
Turn back the page to the yesterdays
When things were bliss and frolicking ways

No one to talk to, no one to hear
If they only knew my inner fear
It tears so hard at my soul each beat
I know I need someone, something, to treat

Hear me oh hear me my cries are quiet
I yearn for help, but want no riot
So how can they know I'm in need?
When bottled up inside is my lonely creed

Courage I need to release my soul
Admit the weakness that creates the whole
Please help me quiet the cries within
Find me a way to stop the tailspin

YESTERDAY, TODAY
& TOMORROW

If I could change my yesterdays into tomorrows
All my todays would be perfect
My yesterdays create my todays
My today defines all of my tomorrows

Reflection is to my yesterdays
As reality delineates all my todays
Hope and wonder frame my tomorrows
But it's all three that shape my presence

I need to make each day be better
All based on the ebb and flows of yesterdays
I hope tomorrows yield is great
But I only control my own todays

So yesterday's create the past, experience grows to always last
Today's rollout the future path, each step unsure, but truly taken
Tomorrow holds the vast unknowns, both good and bad, time will tell
So I need them all these days all told, my yesterdays as they unfold

POWER OF ME

Behold the threshold within, power of me
I hold the throttle to my being
The velocity of my soul rages at my control
Set sail at a whim, no holds barred

It is I that controls me, no one else
My dreams are free, no boundaries, no limits
Boundless and free, guided only by what can be
Not stifled by rules and hazy directions

What holds my power, what depresses my will?
What governs my freedom, my actions on whole?
Who questions my dreams, my boundless desires?
I hold the key to set my soul free, power of me

Truth be told it's always been me
Just a little untidy, unwieldy, and guarded
Scared to push the bubble of if, it, is
Dreams subside back unto and in me, just the power of me

ON A WHIM AND A WHISPER

Twas on a whim and whisper I pondered the night
Nothing but nothing was all in my sight
So jump to the moon, latch on to a star
It's on a whim and a whisper that will take you that far

Whim's take a chance no bet to be clear
Its guts and guile that second the fear
Jump my son, jump to be free
It's on a whim that we stretch our soul with much glee

Whisper so softly not to let it break out
Keep my plan dear to me, no one knows I'll shout
My whisper my whim, my dreams will burst
It's on a whim and a whisper that drives my thirst

Carry me on these whims so tight
Whisper my dreams, til dawn's daylight
Wake the whims of my soul and make them so real
That all of the whispers will live with my zeal

For it's on a whim and a whisper I set my new path
My only hope, not to unleash my wrath
So my dreams are the whims I wish to live
My whispers are words that I truly give

WHO IS MCGOOGITTY?

Someone just asked who McGooGitty was
They asked what is McGooGitty's cause
Is he short, is he tall, is round, is he thin
Just where and how does McGooGitty begin

McGooGitty's no one that you can see
He's someone you've just got to be
McGooGitty's laughter and fun on the run
He's dances and skips through the days humdrum

Reach down inside when life gets you down
McGooGitty will take you for a night on the town
Quaint drinks and laughter will fill the air
All the doldrums' and sadness will soon be fanfare

McGooGitty's in us when we need him the most
So when things get down and you're needing a toast
Reach inside for McGooGitty to bring you some cheer
Share your McGooGitty to friends near and dear

MCGOOGITTY'S TAPESTRY

Ah McGooGitty dances on cobblestone streets
Laughing and slapping all the people he meets
Stranger to no one, friend from the past
Its McGooGitty's spirit that grips us at last

McGooGitty gives us the drive and the fight
To never give up our dreams in sight
Drink up, drink up a pint to your dreams
Laugh O'Leary it's just what it seems

McGooGitty says smile and give cheer
It makes life better for all to hear
So dance on your tip toes my friends and my foes
Today is the day anything goes

For McGooGitty's inside each and every one of us
It's the spirit within that unleashes the fuss
Live happy each minute, each breath that you take
Just think of McGooGitty for everyone's sake

JUST GIVE ME A MCGOOGITTY

Down in the dumps my head wallows and rolls
Give me another this swill my head tolls
Drink my sorrows to depths of despair
Further and further I sink this affair

I need McGooGitty to rescue my soul
Its laughter and chatter to quiet the troll
McGooGitty's the spirit to rest my soul free
Sing loud and clear McGooGitty's in me

Drink lads, drink up, to laughter as one
Together we bond tight as was spun
McGooGitty told me one dark dreary day
Altogether as one, we'll surely play

Drink up, drink up, cheers to your inners'
We're nothing more than McGooGitty beginners
But toast we shall to glad thoughts and dreams
Never they will to quiet are screams

McGooGitty's in us forever to stay
This I know and will surely pray
Just as I write this sad old letter
Tomorrow will just always be better

WISHES ON THE WATER

———— ❦ ————

Each day awakens with wishes intertwined
One wish I hope will truly unwind
Alas my wish fades as the day grows dark
Another bolus of wishes rushes to the spark

Like the endless rings the droplets make
Water is silent until the quake
Wishes rollout from centers deep down
Only to quell, flatten and drown

Dawn brings still waters, sheen of glass reflects the sky
Morning goes, winds take a toll and luster of glass will surely die
Wishes are a plenty dancing in my mind
I wish just this once they'd be so kind

But no matter how much I wish it to be
My wishes come charging one, two, and three
Just once like the water so still and sublime
I want just one wish to be true this time!

MY SISTER

To awaken each morning and wonder aloud
Thank you God for making me proud
You gave me somethings in my life to address
But how you've made it such a beautiful mess

Three boys I have so proud my soul
The inner sickness takes its toll
But no matter the pain and pity I feel
I'm blessed to have so much to conceal

Each breath I yearn takes all my might
But to hold my grandchildren oh so tight
The pain subsides with laughter and hope
It's my family that guides me up the slope

So yes, it's a mess surely to see
The pain inside that consumes me
But lose I won't each day so prized
I'll smile and laugh but never comprised

So to you God you given me much
Without all the pain I'd miss their touch
Brothers, Sisters, Sons, Moms and Dads
I have truly lived my life so, so glad

SPRING TIME DREAM TIME

Unhurried is the drop of the shimmering icicle
Piercing tips shatter the quiet of the pond
The earth cracks under my every step
Spring has risen from snappish day air

Sound of birds fill the sky
Rustle of leaves unhide the spies
Time of birth and feeling free
Each day anew with unknown gifts

Each blade of grass stretches to feel
Just a touch of sun to make life real
Trees reach untethered heights
Roots dig deep to hold the girth

Its spring again dreams on high
Dream new thoughts of what could be
Oh keep these days so fresh and clean
Be still this path of dreams and hope

Keep fresh the spring time feel within
My face welcomes the warmth and breeze
It is with this renewal that dreams are made
I love spring the feel of new, just one dream to come true

ADDICTIONS

Treacherous steps I take today
No turn unchallenged, no test delayed
Courage I muster from deep within
It's one more try to best the spin

They hover above, under, and in
No escape, no quarter, to shed lights sin
Scream out I may leave little doubt
Vile lives inside my soul I shout

I pray each day my steps are sound
Guide me Lord to foundations ground
My ship thrashes to and fro
There's really nothing new to know

Admit the sickness that dwells in me
Honesty and love please set me free
Pray each day for strength and nerve
That I may conquer this reserve

It grabs my soul so cravings rule
I've got to have it each day so cruel
One day, one step, one breath at a time
With love and family, I will make the climb

The mountain is high and steeply laid
One step at a time, one misstep paid
Steady my feet, my hands reach to hold
Oh God as my guide to this I am sold

SET ME FREE

Unleash me from this inner grip
My core craves a simple outward trip
Rest my sullen spirit from jaws of gloom
I cannot see the light through all the plume

Its cloak and dagger I appear
To make my presence hide the fear
Shake me of this wretched stench
My bones quake against the bench

No inner solace nor gratitude
Frees me from this grip so rude
So look inside my inner being
There's nothing much you're really seeing

But wait! Alas there's something here
In depths downtrodden with layers of fear
A reach from Dante's holy hell
Grasp on to hope and faith's ground swell

I see the light from depths down deep
Climb out I will this dread I'll creep
I'm free from all the stench and fear
I live each breath free and clear

VOODOO RIVER

The treacherous journey starts bottle in hand
Voodoo river is calm this trip be grand
Shove off my mate, down river we float
A drink to the tippler, steady the boat

The water churns below the wake
Each bend of the river the dimmer the take
From bank to bank no port in sight
This wicked river has an evil might

Wind down the river no end to see
Waters pace quickens, another nip for me
The gentle breeze snaps to a gust
Rocked we are, get a grip is a must

From nip to guzzle is the only way
To steady oneself from this wild array
The tide rips the hull with soggy lashes
Swerve past the rocks dodge the crashes

Voices sing through the treetops on shore
They told me be wary of this Voodoo snore
My bottle is empty, no drip for the taking
Voodoo River hushed, but I'm still shaking

CLOUDS

Clouds dash across the sky on high
Dreaming I reach out to brush them away
Each one passes with a fable to tell
My mind is the canvas on which to create
Puffy clouds are fun and free
Rolling here and there creatures everywhere

Dragons, unicorns, knights all for one
Stories change with the rush of the wind
Moutains high and steep appear, each one is so near
Then with a puff they disappear, no cloud, no story
Blue oceans now on high above
My clouds have gone, no dreams at hand

Night brings coal against the stars
No dreams of what could be transpires
But tomorrow rises another day
My clouds return this bright lit day
I'll dream again of what can be
It's really just the clouds I see

Tufts of white plumes abound
Not one makes a sound to note
Float across no hinderance here
Shapes form at whim and whisp
Dream again my canvas unfolds
Life springs forth from drifts on high

CANCER

What dreadful grip you place on me
Hidden evil noshes at lifes blood
Seizes my soul with each breaths flood
I will test the trials and will be free
Remedies are slow to cure
My days are filled with pain and doubt
I question why its me and what it's about
All I covet is one more lifes grand tour
Each night I lay, one thought on my mind
Free me oh Lord from this malicious bond
Awake me now, I'm not ready for beyond
I'll live each day and confront the grind
Truth be told I accept this unwell test
I will conquer my quarry by giving it my best

STILL THE NIGHT

Night beckons as darkness edges across the knoll
Shivers my soul for dream time comes anew
What manner awaits my minds depths tonight
Quiet and still the blackness pitches in

Quell my needs this rested start
Lay me down silently fall off gently
Cool pillow top calms my soul
Covers pulled taught, no breeze blows

Drift away on feathers soft and light
My mind now quivers at dawns daylight
Wait! Dreams door upon me now
Which one to take, spinning falling grasp just one

Dreamworld yanks my inner chain
Follow the trip good and bad
Take me out, tether my soul
This dream is bad which way do I go

Sunlight pierces gaps gone uncovered
I awaken slowly blurred by the ride
Did it happen or not my mind to see
Night brings more treks, dreams await

Still the night rest is a must
Toss and turn, calm will prevail
Embrace the night though darkness rolls
Sleep my son sleep, peace is at hand

KISMET

What lies before me this trek I take
Feelings abound my lifes at stake
Empitness surronds my stubborn style
Where can I go no solice in trial

Wretched thoughts consume my core
Fate belies me to bed this whore
Cradle the sanctum of this lowly pair
Its Kismet I tell you through the crosshair

No one controls this excitable path
Destiny's been written slide by its wrath
Take comfort in knowing one simple thing
Its you that controls your inner being

Stand tall and have courage the journeys ahead
Two ways to do this one not be dead
So shout loud and often for all to heed
You are the one to conquer this deed

Kismet's sunset is yours to steer
Drive through the thicket the end is near
Be strong in conviction true to your heart
When it comes down to it you just have to start

FALLING OFF THE MOUNTAIN

The climb is daunting each working day
Built off experience, I pray to stay
Wealth comes in dribbles with hurdles to clear
Walls seem endless, boundless and shear

Pinnacle in sight, sure footed I stride
Advancement is slow but steady to guide
My grip lessens as levels are reached
I'll stay the course as my father preached

Summit is upon me, my wealth not granted
Earned through sweat and grit supplanted
Steady now I'm on high, I've earned my keep
Restless I grow no time to sleep

Temptation creeps the path tilts unsteady
Wealth gives false refuge, for this I'm not ready
Venture presents mock dreams to hold
Plunge into the bucket of worth be bold

My slide begins downward is steep
I grip and I grasp to hold my keep
As hard it was earned with ease I let go
I guess it's just happened, I'll start over you know

So sorry I am to this tragic end
I've hurt the one I love I must transcend
Forgive me my love I'll make this right
Walk together with me the end in sight

JUST A LITTLE BIT OF HEAVEN

Just a tiny bit of heaven is all I ask
What do I do to measure the task?
Stay true to myself and be kind to all
Castaway temptation both big and small

There's no sidewalk stand to purchase a slice
Heaven's quarter earned that's really the price
Sins give the test each day at hand
Devil plays the chords with his evil band

Just one trifling glimpse of heaven's front door
I'll peek and I'll listen to see the ground floor
Journey to heaven is not nearly free
Earned through giving and being true you'll see

So dream of that slice of heaven above
You won't get there my friend on wings of a dove
For it's you my friend that charters the ride
Steady the course, and stem the tide

For heaven's sanctum is one lofty peak
To garner the ticket your life you must tweak
I pray forgiveness for sins of my past
Pray for me Lord that my ride will last

RAMBLING

Ramble I will, stumble I might
Whatever the dribble my goal is in sight
Trample me down, swallow the swill
I will survive you bet I will
Don't worry my friends my words are a jumble
Be steady or not I'll surely stumble
But hidden in these words so mixed
My story, my being, my self be fixed
Heed not my veiled message of woe
But triumph my song ready the show
May not the poet I long to be
But this is just a taste of me
So follow the words on riddles path
Finally from within I've unleashed my wrath

GIBBERISH

They say these prose are nonsense now
No words to extract meaning somehow
I test these words from soul's dark keep
It's just things I think of when I sleep

So run on from one thought to another course
Post the gibberish show no remorse
My words have meaning only to me
I wish that just one could truly see

Menacing thoughts cry out from within
I wish someone would listen to my chagrin
Scribble and dribble a poet I'm not
But heart felt words I cast the lot

These words to me define my scrap
I've fought so hard to speak to you chap
My minds a puzzle no straight arrows flight
I dream of things to my delight

Father battled demons his plight inside
I don't want to take that deathly ride
So read my slobber and take the test
Try to comprise why I tried my best

DEVILS PARADE

—— ❦ ——

Wicked temptress crushes my soul
Pilfers my innards wretched the toll
March with the devil steps one, two, and three
I rest the clutches to be set free

Mischievous sprite the devil is known
Contrite to consume all the angels have flown
Keep step with the devil or test the resolve
My soul is seceding to his quest dissolve

Wait! Lay haste to the wings that soar above
Reach to the sky break from grips of foxglove
Mount the wings of the angel's naps
Ascend to heaven leave all this a snap

Enough is enough this evil charade
Break away, break away, this lonely parade
To hell with the devil I've yielded my part
My soul is my center, listen my heart

Guide me anew let me be set apart
Never, oh never thou tempt me a start
Give no quarter, no sliver, no spec to leak out
I'm done with the devil to this there's no doubt

LIFE'S SUNSET

Skies blister from a heaving sun
My life is lived some facets undone
Birth brings untested treks, sculpts my core
Each day's growth beckons for more

I pass through life's channels, each twist and turn
Days endow the make-up of what defines my yearn
Missteps make best teachings and steady's the path
Grow I will from days gone by, I only desire there is no wrath

Day sun rises from misty grounds
Some days hidden behind a shroud, but life abounds
Temptation licks my soul, stray not from courses laid before
Years wear on my body, each day a weary grasp for more

Sun dips slowly to bed the night
Moon's glow shows so bright
Another day logged life's test passed once more
Tomorrows fair yet to score

I pray tomorrow's sun shines dazzles
I pray no test beats me to a frazzle
For life sunset approach's soon
Breath I will this coming day I will ride on life's balloon

WHEN HAPPINESS DIES

Happiness rings out fills my core
My early youth served this I attend
But sorrow rings and quells the lark
Dad is sick from malady most wretched
Happiness quiet, I wish for delight
Strong I'm asked weather the storm
But days fill with fear my dad consumed
No help comes easy, no writ of a cure
Unto him the cure lives, his happiness dies
Oh happiness's keeper why are you shrouded
What evil coils my father's resolve?
How best to raise this happiness cure
Pray not for miracles to silence the woe
Pray for happiness, pray for hope, pray for my father

JUST A DASH OF SERENDIPITY

———— ❦ ————

Dancing on the midnight street
All the souls I wish to meet
Just one time I hope to see
A tiny bit of luck for me

Treasure trove of days gone past
I just want the luck to last
If just once someone shared a thought
It's definitely something to be sought

But nothing comes to thee for free
Not even a dash of serendipity
For the odds of flukes and wishes be won
Takes more than chance to be spun

So play the tune sing with glee
Pray for something to happen you'll see
Wish upon a star I might
I'll grab for luck and hold so tight

So just this once so whimsically
I pray so hard for that dash of serendipity
One chance, one taste, and one test I need
To dam the luck for which I bleed

ODE TO THE HAWKS

On a sheet of glass you'll ready the test
Each game a plan to conquer the quest
One Goal in mind is all you think
Fly on the ice this foe we'll sink

'Q' calls the boys to gather, play as one
Lace up your boots and have some fun
Puck drop is ready, game is at hand
Pat call's the plays, Eddie O steady's the band

It's Toew's and Kaner, Breadman delivers
Youngsters are strong our opponent quivers
Blades slice the ice, rival in sight
Fans cheer their beloved tasked with the fight

Crow guards the gate, no entry to date
Defense is ready, Seab's and Dunc plan their fate
Hammer's been bruised, Hoss has a plan
To our delight they please every fan

So fight on boys, fight on, win one tonight
The Cup is our grail it's all that's in sight
Step on the ice steady the pace
Lord Stanley is watching it's our only race!

PRESENCE

We exist in the now, we endure to grasp each moment
It is being in the here and now that forms our being
Past exists only to reflect on victories and missteps
Times pace is misleading and continually moves forward
There is no hesitation for time, no slowing, and no hiccup
What we do second to second is becomes an imprint of our legacy
Future is defined not by what we did in the past
But what we decide to do that second, our mind jaunts
Being ever present is a clear choice of self
Define yourself by your next thought and resulting action
Hold yourself to new learnings, log them in secure state
Be present with those you touch, no matter how different
Strive to reach out, open yourself to others
Drive your inner self to heights yet unattained, untouched
Live like you never lived that last second
Guide yourself on steady path's keeping step with time
Presence is the only key, only grail to seek
Rest not waking moments, jack up the idle time
Quest to learn each passing tick, lend yourself to outside touch
I myself have left too much drift into the past
Chances only come but once, take heed in each stake
Be present now as in this writing shows
My thoughts are free and flowing now
I just need that touch of presence

CHOICES

Choices are simple and easy to make
Choices come daily make no mistake
The choices you choose mark the next step
Choose the wrong one begin a bad rep

Choices are not given, they're yours surely spent
Make the wrong one and you shall repent
To make good choices reach deep in your soul
Rely on yourself to test the next roll

Every choice you make need not lament
Reflect on the outcome and then repent
Reflect on the deed stand fast in your choosing
Have confidence my friend if not you'll be losing

Surround your choices with fences of surety
For choices get better with one's own maturity
Choices are not made by others for you
You alone make each one this is so true

So ease your mind in the choices a plenty
Each day's choices grow five, ten, and twenty
Conviction comes from within now I'm sure
Each choice you make is yours to be pure

PRISON OF ADDICTION

Rage rips inside my boiling being
Wretched yearns tear my resolve
What prison bars are these?
No metal, no cold, no rigid sight
My mind strains to quell the quake
Reach out to emptiness, claw and snatch, nothingness
Its emptiness that I bring back, but reach I do
Hold my blinding ravenousness pains
Addictions tears at walls of my heart
What pardon lies ahead for me
Oh God, Oh God, come help me now
Free me from this living hell
Why me, what wish did I tend and get
Treading in this pool of guilt
I reach for a glimpse of shore to gain
But alas this penance is for me to test
Each day anew, fight on within
Tear my soul, thrust pain to friends
I am alone, my freedom wains
Compulsion is my only vet
Calmness lies in the taste of evils cup
I cannot shake this tightening grip
I must sleep, it's the only rest, take me please
My God, My Lord, I trust you'll forgive my weakness
I pray for the piercing pains to soften
One day at a time, one step unsure
I will make the gates of peace open
Receive the sinner, absolved and unsoiled
But first the days quest is still at hand, fight on, fight on

STAR GAZER

Black canvas spread on night's frame
White spec's dot the opus, flickering, dancing, untamed
Pierce the night is one so bright
Marks the start of my star sight
Names are given sure to see
From Taurus, Pisces, Aries, name three
Dream of life upon one star
I toss a wish carry it far
Each star a story, each night there's more
Gazing upon this speckled mass, just one begins my lonely lore
Come dance upon the black lit stage
Each star a player that calms my rage
Star gazing is a release for me
No rules, nor boundaries, I can be free
So gaze upon the stars together
Each star linked just like a tether
The canvas changes every night
Stars will take a different flight
So in my solace let me dream
Maybe I'll catch a ride on one star's gleam

TELL ME I WON'T BE ALONE

Assembled in this lonely cavern
Each second passes abandoned in this swill tavern
No one to speak no wretched whores
I drift on currents ripped far from shores
Please tell me as I waft alone
That you'll be there to help me settle my tone
Loneliness consumes my inner soul
No one to talk with no bell to toll
Stripped of comfort I just lay
Wrapped in blankets of strewn hay
Please hold me tight don't let me go
I crave the solace of one I know
But alas the emptiness is my shroud
Reach I try call out to the crowd
My tears come freely but none to see
I wish each day this prison I'm free
But alone I'm not each day's trial tests
Ocean swells lifts me to the crests
Drowning in this sea of seclusion
Rest this grip of despair give me resolution
Tell me I won't be alone
I'll wait and grind at life's millstone
Promise me you'll be there true
Hold me, hug me, and caress me through
I realize now that alone is a choice
It's really God that has the voice
Trust in him is the only way
Alone you're not with him I pray

CANCERS CURSE

Wretched scourge consumes the flesh
No cure to quick, pain grips the mesh
Each breath sucks vitality from my being
My body weakens, my beauty fleeing
Each move I make raises my fear
Is it deaths door that grows so near?
One thing throughout this vile fight
Is my souls focus on Heaven's sight?
But today I'll whip this evil spirit
It's the day's long match to finally clear it
It devours my bodies' structures for sure
But mind will never succumb, only to cure
Arise from this bed of sickness and waste
Beat this nasty tool remove this aftertaste
It takes my body from the scrap
Rest so easy from this stopgap
My mind, my soul is yours to keep
I'm in heaven now as you sleep

CASTLE OF LOVE

Come upon the castle devout your love to me
Together we'll share our inner amity
My castle is strong and mighty I'm told
Surrounded by towers of love from the bold

Feel safe in your heart walls thick with my care
Never downtrodden nor worried to beware
I'll protect you my darling from any stray suitor
My love I'll teach as your delightful tutor

The drawbridge will drop to let your love in
Entry is grand to my open arms this love begins
Four corner towers protect our love
Released each day is one golden dove

The garden has roses of my undying devotion
We'll walk hand in hand as one in motion
Lay down with me now we'll wish upon stars
The stories they tell will be in our memoirs

This fortress of love is no prison take note
But a home and a life of which I just wrote
I love you more than time can tell
Know my love for you by each ring of the bell

So walk with me, talk with me and let me kiss your soft lips
Each moment endearing like the harbors tall ships
Please tell me you love me, tell me so dear
This castle of love is our whole sphere

ON THE WINGS OF AN ANGEL

Just one time I'd like to fly on the wings of an Angel
Just one time I'd like to feel the heartbeat of Angel wings
One ride with the cherubim is all I wish
My life's complete with one soaring trip on the wings of an Angel
Carry me, carry me to heaven above
Let me soar on the wings of the angel's true love
Take flight and rest easy on the archangel's naps
Soar through the sky shredding the clouds
For love is the fare you pay for the ride
On the wings of an Angel surely you'll glide
Wings of an Angel carry me over the woes that vex me
Earning a trip on the wings of an Angel doesn't come easy, often or free
Angel's appear as light shining bright, dancing on stars to heavens delight
So reach out and catch a ride on this winged carriage
Carry me, carry me to heaven above
Let me soar on the wings of the angel's true love
Take flight and rest easy on the archangel's naps
Soar through the sky shredding the clouds
For love is the fare you pay for the ride
On the wings of an Angel surely you'll glide
Raphael and Gabriel line up your widespread wings
Fly me to heaven pass the flight of the eagle
On your wings I am free to be always me
Guide me, protect me, to heavens purity gates, on wings of an Angel

DEPTHS OF DESPAIR

Free me from this darkened prison
Light slivers pierce my mind's eye
Deliver me from this petulant mood
Each day a trek to stand upon this earth

Exhausted from my minds whirlpools
Deeper I fall into crevices of my mind
No damper to this steepening drop
No peace for my soul, no calming recess

Free me now from gates of hell
Addicted to the deafening wretchedness
Cry out, cry out, no sound heeded
Alone, empty, thoughts echo unanswered

End this twisting, shocking mind game
Discharge me from this whore of doubt
Nausea churns within me, thought creates ill
How to cure this nasty curse

Why me what have I done
Internal tenure of torture pangs
No one hears my silent screams
But one release, no nerve, no resolve, do not end it.............. "

DANCING ON TREETOPS

Dancing on treetops seems easy to me
Tiptoe from branches just one, two, three
No care in the world tippy tap, tippy tap
The world is my playground it's just a snap

So prance along greenery, sprig to sprig
A song in my heart, feet light as a twig
Oh dancing on tree tops gives me delight
Princess and pauper come enjoy my new sight

Wind whips the branches to and fro
Come watch my leaps from down below
Fall I won't my bounds are sure
But don't miss a beat or it's all a blur

Come dance with me, dance with me, and share my glee
We'll hold hands together for all to see
For its dancing on treetops that wishes come true
Just give it a chance and try something new

Treetops and dancing a mix surely meant
If we dance all day we'll be surely spent
But daydreaming gives me the chance to be free
It's dancing on treetops where I want to be

WHEN I WAS A KID.....................

When I was 5 I dreamed to be
Just a bit taller than those around me
Not be scared at the school bus stop
Just to get home from this days long slop

When I was 10 I dreamed to be
The best baseball player for all to see
Fastest on my bike in any days race
It was my goal to be in first place

When I was 15 I dreamed to be
Just safer each day from bullies near me
Fastest one running is how I was known
In with the tough guys when I was grown

When I was 20 I dreamed to be
Just a bit smarter for Dad to see
Thoughts of being a doctor crossed my mind
But study and books were hard to find

Now I'm 60 and dreams fade
I hope what I've done is no charade
Oh being a kid was really long ago
When I was a kid...........................

INSPIRE ME

Inspire me with words of depth
Inspire me to reach beyond
Inspire me to grow up true
Inspire me to tell the truth
Inspire me to love all races
Inspire me to live my dreams
Inspire me to shed a tear
Inspire me to help someone
Inspire me to learn each day
Inspire me to respect all others
Inspire me to question why
Inspire me to create
Inspire me to innovate
Inspire me to say I'm sorry
Inspire me to make mistakes
Inspire me to embrace my fears
Inspire me to share myself
Inspire me to til death is near
Inspire me to be like you
Inspire me to pray to God
Inspire me to inspire someone
Thank you for inspiring me!

SHATTERED DREAMS

My head rests softly on my cool pillow
Breeze blows crisply through the weeping willow
My body grows still, quiet between cool sheets
Eyes heavy with the days tired beats

Dream door opens, what chapter tonight?
Will I be a hero or swallowed by night fright?
Drifting in dreamscape, no ground to set foot upon
Plots flash in mind's eye, which one to choose come-on

My body seizes, quakes, then still
What shattered this calming cool chill?
Running to nowhere, scared beyond measure
This dream has no end, surely no treasure

Run to morning, when is sleep time over
Wake me please, take this dream let me flyover
Twist and turn, please be fake
This cannot be my minds take

Calming softness of cool bed sheets
Soft side of the pillow soothes dream streets
Time to wake, breeze still blows
This dream I had no one knows

PATHWAYS

Pathways are countless so many to choose
Which path starts the ramble, what direction to test?
Life's teachings complete, lead on with no jest
Have conviction in your trials, you've paid all your dues
Trust in oneself is all you should carry
Pathways lend excitement and new horizons to bare
The direction you choose is your only fare
Pathways of life are sewn with newness, yet be wary
Temptations are hidden down pathways soon walked
Missteps are a given, righting the ship is the key
Steady your gate, step gently astride the beach pea
Remember your teaching in how we all talked
The pathway you've chosen is yours to own
So think twice on the direction your outcomes take
It's the legacy you leave on this pathway you make
That will tell your life's story and how strong you've grown
Pathways downtrodden with scars and poor blight
Are signs of misguided and misled doomsdays flock?
Avoid this pathway for sure it's a crock
Your journey is true when sunlight guides your sight
My pathway has been rocky, no smooth waltzing dance
I've strayed too many times from which I was driven
But now I have learned that nothing is given
I stand on my path praying for one more life's chance

THE ALPHABET

A is for Attitude positive, straight and true
B is for Blessings many I pray come soon
C is for Challenges for which I hope I am up to
D is for Desire to always do my best
E is for Enthusiasm for life each day
F is for Forgiveness for wrongs upon me
G is for Goodness I wish upon others
H is for Humor for laughter makes us well
I is for Ideas the ones I can make work
J is for Judgement that I use discretion on others
K is for Kindness to all of my fellow man
L is for Love bestowed upon the throngs
M is for Misdeeds I hope for only a few
N is for Nurturing those that need assist
O is for Optimism that life will be rewarding
P is for Praying that I need to do more of
Q is for Quitting that I never give quarter
R is for Resilience in all that I do
S is for Sincerity in my words and thoughts
T is for Tenderness when times are tough
U is for Unique that I stand out among the rest
V is for Voracious in efforts I endure to accomplish
W is for Wanting to always give my all
X is for Xylophone music sweet and paced
Y is for You that I meet all your wishes
Z is for Zealous in my approach to my life

FATHER MY FATHER

Father my father you left yet too soon
Lessons of life you left me to learn
Oh father why have you left when I willfully yearn
Your teaching falls short, your lessens I bloom
Your teachings to me so young and impressed
Why leave me now at times so dire
You have to stay, you know you're my sire
I wonder and dream yet feel so distressed
What sickness has gripped my hero so true?
I've listened and learned your teachings so dear
Sometimes I wish you were just really near
Its days without end that I am so blue
The journey I take is now taken alone
I wish you were here to listen to my song
But alas it is true you are truly gone
I gaze to the heavens where you've surely flown
I wish and I dream of what could have been
If only you can see what good I have done
My family has grown all of us simply as one
I wish you'd return, I know not when
Oh father, my father your trip not meant
I live as I think you'd want me to be
Its life simple dealings that really make me
I hope and I pray nothing is ill spent

ONE TEAR

One tear I shed from this man's eye
One tear runs down my cheek so weathered
My tears well up from inner dam woes
Tears are not a sign of weakness within
Tears are signs of admitting one's limits
One tear is all it takes to share
All pent up sins that fester the soul
Why so hard to shed one tear
Why so easy to hide the ills
A tear frees up the nested spiral
Share one tear for those that you love
Comfort lies in truths be told
A tear is the key to rest them free
Fear not the tear from which it comes
Fear the tears held from running
One tear to shed for each misgiving
One tear to free life's unknowing moments
So cry on free and revel the ease
Of these tears within you now
Shed one tear with someone you love
Shed a tear for God above

WHEN MY HERO FADES

My newborn eyes look upon my heroes heaving chest I rock at every breath
So soft and caring these gentle giants hands, they caress me, they keep me
Hold me close, I sleep in quiet solace, I have no fear o'er me
I walk with my hero two strides to his one
He protects me from unwanted harm that frightens me
Oh colossus hero lift me to the stars above, pluck one star for me today
Awake!! But not my heroes gone, no titan's gate to gaze upon
Where has my hero gone to be, I look everywhere none to see
Hero fades as day gives to night, all alone creeping fright
My champion's succumb to a hostile fate
Heroes cannot be defeated! So what evil's deed is dealt us now?
My heroes tattered, worn from the fight
Breaths are short his hands brittle from each days long combat
Older now my year's toll shows on my heavy brow
My hero is gone no breath to be given, no touch to feel
Heroes don't die, nor quit, or give quarter
My hero fades but memories last of hero's days gone by
So to you my father my hero supreme
You will always be my hero for days on end
Rest easy in your hero's grave be comforted that I am the hero now

SECRETS

Shhhh, my secrets are quiet within me
Do not awake these many things I've kept so close
Secrets come in many shapes, I keep dire ones silent
Do not even think to expose my noble few
My secrets? Not a lie to me, just private thoughts of truth
Bare no witness to my thoughts, kept safely in hearts lock box
Some secrets I will take and keep, no light of day shall they seek
Others I may choose to share, delight to some, spite to a few
Secrets can consume my flesh, weigh heavy on my humble mind
To share the secrets that devour me, means telling noble truths
But alas I must keep these secrets in, be they all my deepest sins
What wretched fate have I wrought, by quelling these eerie things?
Oh God release these evil riddles, bring peace to my tormented soul
Beware that when these secrets flee, those I love will now know me
Sorry to have kept these close to vest, I've tried to find the right words
So now I know what has to be, secrets have really beguiled me
So be strict in your secret choosing, speak first of troubles true
Share your secrets with one you love, even to God above
End time is near no more secrets to share, too many I hold
I wish I would have shared a few, but no one to hear them told
Why did I gather the lot, secrets were treasured once, now nothingness
Oh why, oh why, my secrets pulse, to die alone, no gift be shared
Take this last secret from my tired lips, I meant no harm, no pity, no foul
Absolve me from these vile mysteries, free my soul unto the sleep

HOMELESS

Of twisted garb and tattered boots
My bones weary from each day's unchartered trek
Each step I take no purpose afoot, rest is rare under a bridge deck
Chased away from each roads corner, who are these evil men in suits
Of days gone passed of which I was, just a dreamer of things to come
Now my toils are all I have, I beg for trifles, scraps and bits
No God above to shine the way, each day's the same this is the pits
No shower to cleanse the day's disease, just the pending noonday scrum
No work, no food, no drink to pass, I reach out my hand for pennies
to take
Please help, help me, this unguarded prison I roam
I'll sleep tonight with one eye open, the devil comes this hidden gnome
Awake the dew seeps across my face, another day of my heartache
Pardon me from this desolate destiny, show me how to be free
Again I pray to those that pass, this alas was not my plan
My heart still beats, my breath is parched, and this today is my
life's span
Look upon these rags I bare, see through the torn façade, it's me!
So lay me in that unknown grave, sleep softly, and sleep still
Peace at last, my journey ends, what purpose to post
I've forgotten all the needs I had, I forgot the family I miss the most
Rest assured your torture ends, God will hold you this his will

TAKE IT TO THE GRAVE

Light dims, end is near, cold cloaks my frame
So much to divulge, so much to claim
What do I do? How to make amends, less woes?
Who to tell? So many friends and foes

Unmask these hidden appalling truths be told
Carried the burden so long, I'm so old
Hell lives within this body's wall
I've spared my loves this pitted sprawl

Release the voice deep in the well
Truth shouts out bid fond farewell
Stop! heed not the devils cries
To reach the promise of this compromise

Confess your sins, let truth's ring out
Release the weight of guilt and doubt
To your grave your journey halts
Bury me with all my faults

So as I lay down to sleep
Rest assured this I will keep
Of nasty truths I will not crave
I took them all to my grave

WALK TALL MY SON

Unsteady footsteps a child's gate
Walk steady on oceans of green, green grass
Each step anew, unsure in this seemingly endless morass
Stride true and grasp each tempted debate
Grow my son have faith in your measure
Stand tall to those who question your resolve
Etch lessons of life as you evolve
Never give quarter nor surrender your treasure
Walk tall my son through thick and through thin
Each day is a blessing God's gift to your lore
Your children you'll teach this you cannot ignore
So step assured that this is where you begin
For life's simple lessons begin with one step
Walk tall my son tall, for this is your fate
Grind out each day as if it's your last
Look out to the future not much on the past
For if you heed these words you'll surely be great

THE LAST CALL

O' Father your vexed journey's end nears
O' Father you've missed so much these years
O' Father how much I wish you were there
My Father I wish I could have shown how much I care

The pain of waiting that last call
The journey's end after that long haul
What dreadful days you surely spent
Time must have lingered but not as it meant

Miles between us I cannot be there
Minutes are like hours waiting on a prayer
We've made the tontine to let you go on
May God guide you anew to that beyond

Hold those slim memories of early days past
Your suffering is over your comfort at last
We know you loved us one in all six
The cure you seek is this, the only fix

We've been given the deed to let you pass
Why I'm the one to do this I'll pray at next mass
Oh God please forgive me for letting him go
Find peace in heaven that's all I surely know

BROTHER

My brother by blood, my best friend in life
Though younger and eager you strike away my strife
You've given me so much, so much I can take
Never leave me my brother, stay true to our stake

Laughter is our mantra, no sadness is sown
Each time we are near I feel like I've grown
Come often, come early and we'll tip a few
My comfort is your company this is nothing new

A Scotch I will have always your brew
We'll laugh till our hearts ache this we can chew
Jokes a plenty no kidding aside
We'll take our life together once and astride

But I know if I need you and the chips are down
You'll be there to lift me up off the letdown
Come hold me and help me we'll cry as we're one
My strength will be solid because we're not done

Oh brother you've meant so much to be sure
I cannot imagine a life without you unsecure
So thank you my friend for who you truly are
Together we'll get there no matter how far

THE ARRIVAL OF
CHARLOTTE QUINN

Sweet Charlotte first slumbers end is near
Arrival soon sweet and dear
What waits you soon is love and care
You will be delivered on angel's prayer

So many to hold you and guide your life's quest
What waits for you now is surely the best
Who will you be our Charlotte Quinn?
No matter our love, love counts within

Days pass by, angels note pings my ear
Charlotte's arrival is now here
God has blessed our families true
Oh God she's so precious and so new

Who will you be our tiny Charlotte?
You will be our little starlet
I hold you now so tiny, so sweet
You've taken our hearts on every beat!

NO MORE TEARS

Know my heart through tethered verse
Allow my silent thoughts disperse
Rid my strife through troubled times
Yearn for the sound of angel's chimes
No more struggles, no more tears
Behind me now my daily fears
Each day I pray for those I love
All I ask on the wings of a dove
To you my Lord I come now free
Your prayer is answered now I see

ONE LAST BREATH

—⟨◦⟩—

Each breath I take I wonder once more
Last one forever or another encore
Each step a trial to extend my days
I've done all my penance through daily haze
My body the subject of malady's gone past
Just how much longer will each day last
Each ride in the wagon to no cavalcade
Mend me for a time, another charade
One day closer is how I now tell
Seems like truly I'll never be well
But rest assured friend, I truly hear
All the good you have spread and loving good cheer
Your memory fixed my mind is now straight
I'm sure and I'm certain you're at heaven's gate
Be calm in knowing your touch has gone deep
May God grant you the peace and much needed sleep

TWISTED TALE

Oh twisted tale of dreadful waste
Steadfast in thought discard all haste
Whilst evening comes night's curtain drops
Wrapped tightly in my sleepy props
Dream takers wait this calm beginning
I'm clearly not the one who's winning
Fall deeper now in conscious well
Grab on so tight the whipping carousel
Bedlam roars I'm pricked and spun
Stop this wicked tales long run
What halts these swirling thoughts of lore?
Its tale stay twisted no lie to ignore
My dreams of peace and happy times
Softly dwindle like windless chimes
Evil is what evil does, twist the tale of my dreams gate
As hope dims out on thoughts of hate
Awake me now to mornings light
Take me from this nightly fright
I can't, I won't sleep away, sleep away
Spare me from this awful foray
Just once to sleep on peaceful yarns
Warn me, test me just ring the alarms
Wait my son wait, there's doom in night's sleep
So heed my warning, wade slowly and quiet into the deep

LIVE'S WE LEAD

Look back upon this life you've lead
Each step taken a seed been sown
My daughters, my son, continue this lore
Life's great venture you cannot evade
Take solace in knowledge each day presents
Spread your wings and take the leap
You have the gift of life's fresh breath
Take not some of the ill laden path's I trampled
Stay true to the path that you alone create
Each step a journey, a risk, a reward
Always move forward, love and friendship your guide
Truth wins out in life's sweet game
No measure surrendered, no evil shall bleed
Life can be easy, blessings abound
So heed this warning of which I'm to speak
Love is the answer you always seek
Its friends and its family that levels this trek
Trust in them and your life will be grand

THE GAME CHANGER

What's the time when the game's on the line?
What is it when all is lost, so we whine?
Who do we need to turn the tide?
Who's the hero who takes the stride?
There's only one that it can be
Only one we're meant to see
They're the Game Changers who we'll call
The one that crashes that big stern wall
They surpass normal states of being
They do the things we can't believe we're seeing
They're not big, mighty or strong
They just meet the rushing throng
The moments presence is how their made
No challenge to big, no lead not swayed
Game Changer's credo is one of winning
There is no spec of defeat while they're grinning
They carry it with them but you cannot see
They stop the crowd, enter the grand prix
You too can be a Game Changer this bright new day
It just takes your spirit, your mind, your heart
If you need to win one true, step up, step up give it a start

LOOKING THROUGH
THE TIGERS EYE

⸺ ❧ ⸺

Seeing with the Tigers eye inner self be found
The Tigers eye is strength defined
Of confidence and power thou must be refined
Prosper from the boost around
The Tigers eye clears illusions blur
Center your eye on Chakra's goal
You're will, your drive, your inner soul
Look deep within without a stir
The Tigers eye seals your might
The core is the secret goal you seek
It's you inner power you will tweak
The Tigers eye protects your egos plight
Take pleasure from the power within
Use the Tigers eye to all's chagrin

DEPTHS OF MY WORDS

Do not just skim over these humble words I've authored
These words are more than a simple diatribe of life
These lexes are the key to the inner soul
Each phrase exposes the depths of truths untold
Bare not false witness to these verities
Accept these truths from triumphs and failures
Life unfolds a journey unplanned
I stand before you tested and tame
I've ridden life's waves to heights of dreams
I've crashed under the weight of a wave
Life deals many an unknown and wary hand
I've met some challenges and failed some grand
So heed these simple prose I pen
Hidden treasures can lie within
Take some solace that now you know
The depths of my being I shall not show

FACES

So many faces pass me by
So many wonder who am I
Just one face I wish to know
Each face I pass simply pale to the sky

Where do all the faces go?
These faces fade from here and there
What story they carry on their brow
Each one I pass I know not where

Some faces glance a nod my way
Some hide their anger from whence they scurry
I wonder what they see in mine
I wonder if the feel my worry

It's only I that knows the face I seek
The face of peace and life sublime
Where is this face of hope I need
What keeps this face away sometime?

I pass a window, stop! That face I see
Can it be the face I see?
Step close, look hard, why that face
It's, it's really just me!

JOURNEY THROUGH
THE ROSES

Do not rest on roses stem?
Keep climbing to the red pedals of heaven
Grab the prickly rod and rise
Make each step sure and steady
The rose's beauty is not without risk
Ride the rose on the day's brisk wind
Trust the softness of the pedals strength
Rest your head on the closed rosebud
When daylight comes rise with wonder
Feel sun's warmth as the rose rises
The ride is short and filled with peril
For a roses life is not an endless one
Its days are numbered and it's wonder short
So journey through the roses when life is full
Revel in the life of fullness
Complete the cycle each day you live
Cause roses give you but one chance
To see, to feel, to smell the beauty
Relish that chance each breath you take
We only get to journey in life sometimes

PEEK-A-BOO DANCER

What's a peek-a-boo dancer you ask me to see?
Peek-a-boo's are everywhere step one, two and three
They rock and they wiggle to anyone's tune
Just pay attention and you'll see one soon

On the train, on the bus, on the sidewalk for sure
They tiptoe on lily pads they can't help find a cure
So where oh where is a peek-a-boo dancer
They're right in front of you my friend you have the answer

They sport buds and listen to all kinds of jingles
Watch their legs and their feet and oh derrières
They dangle and wobble to some crazy tune
Not a care in the world who's watching their swoon

Some giddy some ditty, some surely real square
But I swear if you don't try it you'll miss a dare
So I can't help but feeling that everyone here
Is a peek-a-boo dancer just look and beware!

RISE UP

Rise up from your births start scramble
Draw in the air that starts life's ramble
First step you wobble, unsteady without aid
Rise up and reach out to life's unknown be played

Rise up each day to mornings light
Stand tall to the coming untested plight
For within you is the resolve to conquer your fear
Rise up no armor, no weapon near

Rise up as only you can do
Heed not the temptations often and new
Slay the day's dragons as you grow
Rise up I say as only you will know

Rise up and seize your manhood's grail
For you have slain the gauntlet's trail
Your wisdom comes from days gone past
Rise up and make each new day last

Rise up and live your destiny full
Lock on the steely eyes of the bull
For you have completed your journeys trip
Rise up once more you've steadied the grip

PONDER LAKE

Wherever I am, wherever I go,
I'll just closes my eyes and see Ponder Lake
It's blue and pristine ever so quiet
My thoughts are the crafts that sail upon it
I'll gather them all in one great fleet
I'll mount an assault on evil thoughts charging
The breeze blows swiftly but gently to feel
No quarter given, no ominous loss
Ponder Lake is the refuge that is my grand home
The water slaps softly on sand white as snow
No whitecaps or waves to unsteady my thoughts
So calm am I now all is forgiven
My missteps forgotten for even a moment
Solitude surrounds my body and mind
No breach of this fortress I'm safe and I'm sound
But one craft approaches across Ponder Lake
It travels from heaven on a silken wake
I'll take a ride on that golden ship
Because peace is upon me for this there's no wait

JUST ONE TIME

Just one time to be first
Just one time to quench my thirst
Just one time to be right
Just one time to win the fight
Just one time to have my prayer heard
Just one time to have the last word
Just one time to get that smile
Just one time not to wait a long while
Just one time to be seen
Just one time to not be mean
Just one time to stand up tall
Just one time for you to catch my fall
Just one time to share what love is
Just one time to pass the quiz
Just one time to not have to ask
Just one time to put down my mask
Just one time I wish I'd be
Someone you want just being me

MIRROR MIRROR EVERYWHERE

Mirrors are at every turn you see
Mirrors are reflective to my chagrin
Glance around the place your in
You'll see yourself big and small

Behind the bar the mirror shows
The tall beer glass makes you grow
Napkin holder peeks a glimpse
Shiny spoon tells no sin

Door window reflects your mood
Rear view mirror casts your steely eyes
So beware to guide your look
The mirror is that lonesome crook

Mirror tells the truth you know
Mirror does not hide yourself within
Funny thing when we gaze at our self
We cannot hide who we are

So take a moment to be sure
The one you see each day you start
Is someone who you really are
Take a gander look around it's you my friend soon be found

WHEN LAUGHTER DIES

Sad you know when laughter wanes
Living is hard feel the pains
When laughter rises spirit grows
Laughter completes us so everyone knows

Laughter is the cure for your ills
It's what gives us all the thrills
So when darkness creeps upon your brow
Try to reach that silly vow

Strike down the sadness and clouds of woe
Find the hidden cackle to grow
Fight for the truth be told
Never succumb to darkness be so bold

When once upon that dreary time
Mom and I had that inane chime
We left dad at the sawbones for some quick aid
What was so serious we soon swayed?

And laugh we did of good times to come
To some we looked just so glum
But laughter she said cures the pain
Laugh I do when times are bad, this is my true sultry gain

WALKIN' AND STRUTTIN'

Sometimes I'm walkin' down the lane
I break to a step struttin's my game
No one knows my inner glee
Just know for the fact that it's just little ole me
No tune is playin' in my ear
Just a song from yesterday that twists a cheer
So strut with me, walk with me one, two, and three
Be oh so different that they will gape
You're the one that settin' the tone
Touch a heart as you pass your dance step true
Always so perfect, so grand and true
Tippy tap, tippy tap on and off the curb
Balance your toes on life's edge so grand
I'm happy I'm dancin' in my own world
For me it's freedoms victory bell
So just once in a while strut yourself home
And feel so high that life is so full
Just walkin' and struttin' to your own delight
It's what makes you unique in everyone's sight......

AIR GUITAR

Watch me, see me strike up a tune
I'm playing my guitar to you I will swoon
No sheet of melody to play my chords
I'm not going to be on any billboards

But to me I'm like Hendrix, Clapton, and more
Playing to the crowd no numbers galore
But on that stage in my mind's eye
I wow them and amaze them with my battle cry

Next tune on the box and I spin the next mix
Come on baby you know me my axe in the kicks
Rockin away in my own little gig
On the stage I'm a playin' and dancin a jig

I wish I could strum that real guitar
But my friends and family would think that really bazaar
So dream I will with this air made thing
I'm happy to be playing this one last fling

JAKE

His start for life was different from us
No one knew the turbulent womb
He was to be born with struggles from within
Deprived of the riches the air we breathe gives

Each day a fight, a reach through the tremors
But struggle he did with family together
Each step a bit off a tipplers gate to some
The braces they fit impeded his stride

Jake gives no quarter no test to skip past
When they told him he couldn't he already did
Running his races was surely no breeze
Cut and bruised easily, the finish, the goal

Finish he did to the crowd's uproar
For Jake there is no can't, no not trying to do
For college and studying is not easy for him
He conquered the books and tests he did take

No with two sons that heaven has made
Jake conquers it all one step at a time
Give me a little courage just like Jake
With that I will conquer my own simple fate

FACES OF THE MOON

Night falls on grass so bent and still
Looming glow of nights dark window
How many faces of the moon tonight?
What stories to tell as I gaze at the sight

Sliver of the moon speaks stories of fright
Half dotted surface means more delight
Full face of the moon can shed some light
Which face of the moon will I see tonight

I pray upon the moonlit night
Spare me now my self-made plight
Thou aren't beauty at dawns daylight
Share my secrets to moons scared face

The moon is my keeper of my shadows within
I tell no one my secrets at heart
Moon beams search my whimsical path
Faces of the moon be true

A friend I have in moonlit night
There is no shame no childish fright
Come with me now and meet the face
Of moonlit dreams I'll share my story

STRAIGHT SHOOTER

Gimmee the straight shooter
Just cut to the quick
Razor's edge sharp to wit
No sugar to coat the truth I need

Straight shooter will tell me how it is to be
It hurts at times these words so true
Hard to grasp, hard to swallow
But truth it is these simple words

Why so hard to hear each one
Truth cuts to the core no hidden meaning
It's what should have been, it's what I should hear
But why so hard to digest these tales

Give it to me straight no sugar to make these words so sweet
I want the straight shooter to steer my course
Take my hand and pull me through the truth
I cannot stand to hide these things

Truth be told I knew all along
Truth be told no cowards swell tongue
Truth be told just ask me true
I'm the straight shooter, take heed in my skinnies

BLACK SNAKE

Beware the evil and treacherous vibe
Face of softness hides the devils charade
Fangs recoil until ones strikes out
Never be seen, heard or a strike

Eyes dressed in slits for all to see
Reaching out its slow slither and soft disposition
It strikes not with venom but pen in hand
The air smells of niceness

When your guard is down and comfort is high
She strikes with a venom so persuasive and numbing
My stomach is sick from this strike cannot bear
My legs weaken from digesting the tainted diatribe as sold

What, when, how, did this all take place....
Shimmering, questioning this strikes crippling feel
I swear, I swear, nothing is true
Black snake was a sheep so calm and set to

Never trust the eyes of a friend you labor with
Walk tall and speak softly and never do waver
For Black Snakes abound when you never see them
Never in my dreams would this befall me, beware the snake

MCGOOGITTY RISES

— ⤜⤚ —

The story's been told that McGooGitty's in you
But these days of my past he sleeps deep within
I wish he would rise and turn out my grin
If he'd dance and diddle I needn't be blue

So rise up McGooGitty and take me away
Shake my doldrums' from my inner core
Just one more time and break the folk lore
Dance with me, sing with me in a new array

Rise up I say you bastard of joy
So I'll pick a pint up and see if you're there
I swear to the end on a wing and a prayer
So prepare for the night and revel as Teddy boy!

No swill to steady my morbid hells gate
One, two, tap, tap, tap, a dance of the jig
So well up from within McGooGitty's sprig
He rises, I feel him, deep down in one's slate

McGooGitty's rises when I let him wake
No sorrow or sadness will quell his own lot
For we handle McGooGitty's plot
He's there each time, he's there for the take!

HELP MOLD ME

———— ⚬⌇⚬ ————

Cry out from within this wombs prison
The shell I carry hides my beauty's song
A simple mirror helps brush the new mold I need
Transcend this world I struggle to see
I'm looking for one, two, maybe three, allies
Just to be near and tell me I am me
No toughness, no struggle, just casual times
Some call it different, outside the vanilla stream
But dream I will and cackle inside, hold hope so tight
Mold me to who I am, not what you want me to be
I'm open you see to each of you no matter how striking
For it's the you inside that interests me
Treat me like royalty and my kingdom is yours
But take heed on approach I can be coy at first meet
So be firm in your stance, take charge to begin
Patiently teach me, patiently guide me, patiently touch me
　　From these lessons you'll learn my treasure within
　　Like a new flowers blossom, I'll surge to the sun
Make me ideal I am what I am, come kiss me tonight

DUFFER'S DAY

Mist rolls in the morning light
Predawn wake to my delight
I'll slay the course with all my twigs
Hope my game marvels the bigwigs

At the tee box now, two orbs I carry
My Mulligan is ready, neat and wary
Slow the pace, steady the stroke
My brother is watching and ready to joke

I smack the shot with all my might
The flight is long and grand in sight
But alas a turn not planned to see
This one is gone not found by me

So Mulligan it is on the day's first trek
Slow down the pace on golfs flight deck
My brother is laughing too hard to go
I'll show him one time with this mighty blow

Brother is up, all quiet just a low hiss
Swing away!! Swoosh and a miss
Who's laughing now my little boy blue?
Come back we will this all will be new!

FALLING FROM THE
SEVENTH STAR

Start the clatter one pence makes six
Thrill of the roll makes ones heart tick
One more roll this bet be made
I've won again no sad tirade

Platinum level the first stepping stone
Play the marker down to the bone
Gifts start rising as the risk goes higher
Stake gets steeper but the wins catch fire

Diamond elevates the free pass zones
Bet my soul for one roll of the bones
More gifts are paraded my sight to see
All of them grand and seemingly free

Seventh star ascension is the pinnacle I seek
Nights last stay in this Sin City streak
Unwary warnings of the fall soon to bare
Play on, Play on the devil may care

The fall is so hard from the heights of a star
What happened so quickly seemed way too far?
They wine you, they dine you, treat you with fanfare
So to all those that follow be guarded, beware

QUINTESSENTIAL MAN

Who is this man I do not know
What thoughts bare witness to see him grow?
He does the things I long to see
What is that man it cannot be?

So damned am I from his lofty soul
I've tried to climb from the depths of the black hole
How perfect a man just has to be?
The test will come just wait and see

The grail is elusive and hidden about
One way too steady this trophy so stout
So how to be this perfect man
I stand before you no laid plan

Each step I take I try to be, that man who came to be
That man is gone from my journeys' plea
Torn from this world by evils woe
No path to follow, no legacy in tow

You left without filling this lone flask
How do I finish this daunting task?
So how do I become this quintessential one?
You left me father long ago, why you left one and done

DEVILS IN THE SIDE CAR

Kick the engine, rumble and roll
Road ahead twists like the dragon's tail
One's life's journey starts out alone
No guide to point the path one needs

Shift into gear, slow goes the start
Each turn I take this test I make
Into the side car comes the devil be born
Trust him not, I shudder soul rambles on

Take heed he says with that searing red glare
Follow my map and great quests to take
Faster, faster my son should you go
One point of my finger and evil's in tow

Not tonight Mr. Evil, no shrouded plan
Trust my soul, mine to keep
Unleash the side car, set him free
For the devil's price too steep to see

So ride on I go, splendid horizon awaits
My life's choice has got to be great
Spin the wheel, untether the clutch
This life is my choice not really that much

ROCK, RUMBLE, AND ROLL

Just a little rock, just a roll
We'll rumble today until the bell tolls
Come on and party the day's still new
One pop, one fizzle, one turn of the corkscrew

We'll rock, rumble and roll
Rock, rumble and roll
Yeah, yeah, yeah
Just a little rock, rumble and roll

Bottle's empty, hit me again
Pop the top, slide one to Big Ben
Friends all tip one to my chagrin
I'll have another til my head spins

We'll rock, rumble and roll
Rock, rumble and roll
Yeah, yeah, yeah
Just a little rock, rumble and roll

EVILS GRIP

Night falls, secrets kept
Deep in my soul calmly wept
Sun rises, peaks on high
This day alone, reach the sky
What turn awaits my next leap
All my heart for peace and sleep
Wretched ulcer days on end
One more prayer this day I send
Each time I grasp for things to hold
Empty is each hand as told
I dread to lay my head to rest
Fear grows deep, begins the test
But alas the trial rallies anew
Wish and hope fades as blue
Who has this dreaded grip?
I'm tired of this fretted trip
Just once to lay me down I pray
Please leave my soul this blessed day

JUST ONE MORE CHANCE

Just one more chance to right the drift
One more try to live the gift
What's done is done, the story carved
Just one more try, though inners starved

The ship still docked, new course is laid
Captain's soul is how it's played
Crew within my deepest core
Unbound the vessel, depart the shore

One more chance tried and true
Path is given not so new
Alter the path on chances test
Shots been given do your best

One more chance was all I need
Life's been given to do the deed
I'm captains' own the one that be
I run the course just wait and see

Pray these days for one more chance
Pray these nights take one last stance
Captains crew stands tall an proud
I've taken the chance and yelled aloud!

DRIVEN

No stone unsettled,
*   No facet squandered*
Quest for knowledge,
*   Answers not taken*
Tenacious am I,
*   To each given task*
No quarter granted,
*   Willful completion*
Challenge is sustenance,
*   I hunger for more*
No complaints of mass,
*   One step at a time*
Chip away, chip away,
*   Solution be found*
Starved for knowledge,
*   Glutton to learn*
Another charge given,
*   A smile returned*
Learn again, grow again,
*   Each day I ascend*
No victim here,
*   See it, own it, do it*
For she is a wonder,
*   This Carmen, I found*

Printed in the United States
By Bookmasters